ORIOLE PARK BRANCH
DATE DUE *2-03*

SCIENCE
PROJECTS

CHEMISTRY

Chris Oxlade

Photography by
Chris Fairclough

RAINTREE
STECK-VAUGHN
PUBLISHERS

A Harcourt Company

Austin   New York
www.raintreesteckvaughn.com

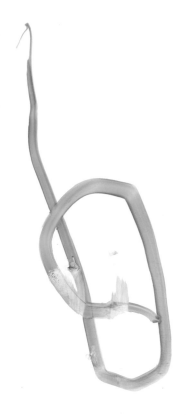

Library of Congress Cataloging-in-Publication Data
Oxlade, Chris.
Chemistry / Chris Oxlade.
    p.   cm.—(Science Projects)
    Includes bibliographical references and index.
    Summary: Introduces the basic concepts of
chemistry through a variety of experiments, exploring
such topics as changes of state, distillation, and
catalysts.
    ISBN 0-8172-4948-6
    1. Chemistry—Experiments—Juvenile literature.
    [1. Chemistry—Experiments. 2. Experiments.]
    I. Fairclough, Chris, ill. II. Title.
    III. Series: Science projects.
    QD38.094 1998
    540'.78—dc21   97-46796

Printed in Italy. Bound in the United States.
  2 3 4 5 6 7 8 9 0 02 01

Picture acknowledgments:
The publishers would like to thank the following for
permission to reproduce their pictures:
Bruce Coleman: pages 20, 28, 37; **Getty Images**: pages
19, 22, 24, 27, 31, 34; **Science Photo Library**: front cover,
pages 4, 8, 13, 32, 38, 44.

Illustrations: Julian Baker: front cover, pages 39, 41;
Stefan Chabluk: pages 8, 10, 13, 21, 28, 34, 42, 43.

CONTENTS

WHAT IS CHEMISTRY?

When you hear the word chemistry, what do you think of? You might think that chemistry happens in a laboratory full of test tubes, Bunsen burners, and bottles of colored chemicals and is done by people wearing white coats and goggles. But most of the things that chemists study happen around us in our everyday lives.

A chemical is any substance that chemists use or make. We use chemicals at home, at school, and at work. We use them for cleaning and cooking, as fuel for our transportation, in factories, in building, and in medicine.

Chemistry is the study of what things are made of, how different substances behave, and what happens when different substances are mixed together. Many chemists study how to manufacture new chemicals. Others find out how useful chemicals, such as fuel for engines, are extracted from natural substances, such as oil.

Many chemicals are dangerous, and even those in your home can be harmful. All dangerous chemicals should have warning symbols on the container, but never touch, smell, taste, or mix any chemicals unless you are sure it is safe to do so.

The typical image of a chemist at work in a laboratory is only a small part of chemistry. Chemistry takes many forms. It happens all around us as substances mix, separate, and change form.

CHEMICAL MAGIC

1. Ask an adult to help you with this experiment. Boil the egg for ten minutes to make sure it is hard-boiled. Allow the egg to cool, and peel it.

2. Drop a blob of modeling clay into the bottle. Press the blob onto the bottom of the bottle with the stick.

3. Make a long tube from the thin cardboard, narrow enough to fit into the bottle. Drop it into the bottle so that it rests on the clay, but don't press it in. This tube will help you to get the candle into position.

4. Drop the candle down the tube. The sides of the tube should help keep the candle upright until you have pressed it firmly into the modeling clay. Then you can turn the bottle upside down and remove the tube.

5. Tape a matchstick to the end of the stick. Light the match and use it to light the candle. Quickly rest the egg in the neck of the bottle and wait. Magically, the egg is pulled into the bottle. Why do you think this happens?

MATERIALS

- a wide-necked bottle
- an egg
- modeling clay
- a birthday candle
- a thin stick
- thin cardboard
- safety matches
- tape

WARNING

- Make sure an adult is present when you are using safety matches.

SUBSTANCES

In chemistry, the word substance means the same as the word material. It can be a chemical (such as salt), a mixture of chemicals (such as concrete), or a natural substance (such as wood). It can be a solid, a liquid, or a gas. There are many thousands of different substances. Some are found under the ground or in animals and plants. Others are synthetic, which we make from natural substances.

Substances have different properties, such as hardness, density, texture, strength, how well they dissolve in water, and how well they conduct electricity and heat. When you describe a substance, you are describing its properties. Knowing the properties of different substances helps us tell one from another.

The properties of a substance make it useful for certain jobs. Wood is a useful building substance because it is easy to cut into shapes, is very strong, and lasts a long time. The metal copper is a very good conductor of electricity, so it is used for electrical cables and other wires. Glass is useful because it is transparent and, in its molten form, can be molded into many shapes.

USING DIFFERENT SUBSTANCES

MATERIALS
- a notepad and pencil

1. Walk around your home or classroom. Look at everything you see, and choose ten different objects.

2. Write down each object's name. What material or mixture of materials do you think the object is made from? Write the names of the materials next to the object.

3. Now think about why those materials have been used, and write down what you think.

FEEL IN A BOX

1. Cut a hole in one side of the box, just large enough for your hand to fit through.

2. Cut a piece of cloth large enough to cover the top opening, and a smaller piece to fit over the hole you have cut yourself.

3. Stand the box on its side, and tape the larger piece of cloth onto the box to form a curtain that drops down over the opening. Make a curtain for the small hole the same way.

4. Ask a friend to put different objects in the box without your seeing them. You have to figure out what the objects are by feeling them through the hole. (You can use the saucer to put liquids in the box.)

5. As you feel an object, think about how you can tell what material it is made of. Is it cold or warm to the touch? If it's cold, it could be a metal. Feel the surface texture. Is it hard or soft? Lift it in your fingers. Is it heavy or light? If the object is synthetic, think about its materials and why they have been used.

MATERIALS
- a cardboard box
- a piece of cloth
- scissors
- tape
- everyday objects with different textures
- a saucer

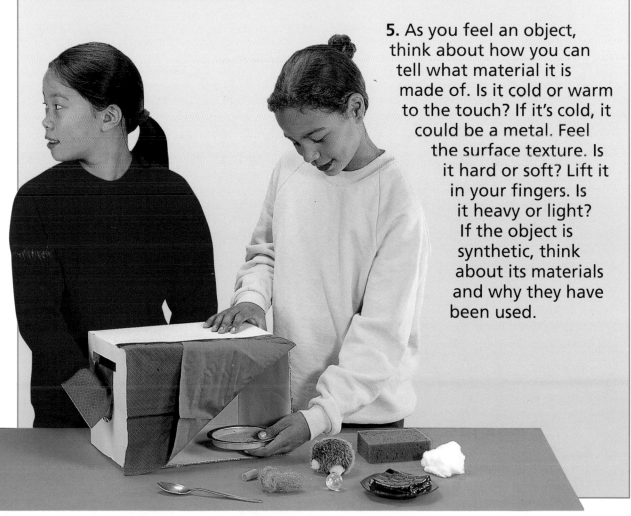

ATOMS AND MOLECULES

All substances are made up of tiny particles called atoms. Atoms are unimaginably small. There are many millions of them in even the tiniest piece of material, such as a speck of dust. Substances are different from each other because they are made up of different types of atoms or different combinations of atoms.

Atoms might be extremely tiny, but an atom is made up of even more tiny particles. At the center of an atom is its nucleus, made up of particles called neutrons and protons. Around the nucleus move electrons. If an atom loses some of its electrons, or gains some electrons from another atom, it becomes an ion.

It is very difficult to split the nucleus of an atom. When scientists can "split" an atom, a huge amount of energy is released. This is used to produce energy in nuclear power plants and to create nuclear explosions.

This diagram shows the differences between an atom, an ion, and a molecule, using chlorine as an example.

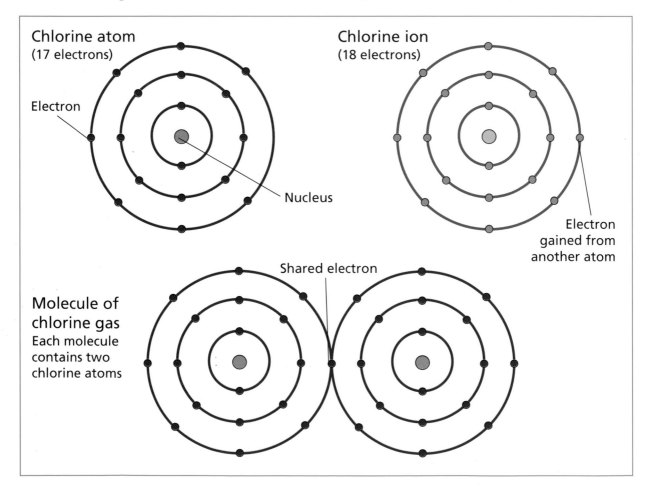

Chlorine atom
(17 electrons)

Electron

Nucleus

Chlorine ion
(18 electrons)

Electron gained from another atom

Shared electron

Molecule of chlorine gas
Each molecule contains two chlorine atoms

Some substances, such as metals, are made up of identical atoms. Others, such as salt, are made of different ions. Still other substances are made up of molecules. A molecule is a group of atoms joined together. Some molecules contain just a few atoms. Others contain hundreds of atoms in long chains.

The kind of particle a substance is made of can determine its properties.

For example, materials with small molecules of only one or two atoms are normally gases at room temperature.

DID YOU KNOW?

An atom is mostly made up of empty space because the electrons are far away from the nucleus. If the nucleus were the size of a pinhead, the atom would be 33 ft. (10 m) across!

THE SIZE OF MOLECULES

1. Fill a shallow dish with water.

2. Gently sprinkle talcum powder onto the water surface. Blow away any excess to leave a thin film. Gently stir the water to break up the film, but don't mix the powder into the water.

MATERIALS

- a shallow dish
- lubricating oil (not cooking oil)
- talcum powder
- a drinking straw
- a ruler
- a spoon or small stick

3. Dip a drinking straw into some oil. Hold your finger over the top end and lift the straw out. Let a drop of oil fall from the straw into the dish by taking your finger off the straw's end. The tiny drop spreads into a huge patch. The patch is just a few molecules thick.

STATES OF MATTER

Substances can be solids, liquids, or gases. These are called the three states of matter. Look around you and you will probably see only solids. But remember that the air that you are breathing is a gas, and that not far away there will be water, the most common liquid on Earth.

The main difference among solids, liquids, and gases is the way that the particles (atoms, ions, or molecules) are arranged and joined together. In a solid, the particles are closely packed together in a regular arrangement. The particles vibrate, but cannot move from one place to another. In a liquid, the particles are still quite closely packed, but they can move around. In a gas, the particles are widely spread and can move around freely.

These properties mean that solids have shape, liquids flow into the bottom of the container they are in, and gases expand to fill the container they are in. Solids and liquids can change shape, but cannot be squeezed into a smaller space, as gases can.

In many solids, the particles are arranged in a neat, regular pattern of shapes, called crystals. The pattern gives a crystal its overall shape.

CRYSTAL SHAPES

1. Cut some pieces of stiff cardboard on which to build your crystal shapes.

2. Attach a small piece of putty or modeling clay to the marbles to hold them in place when you put them on the cardboard.

3. Using the marbles to represent atoms in a crystal, build the three shapes shown here.

MATERIALS
- marbles or round wooden beads
- sticky putty or modeling clay
- stiff cardboard
- scissors

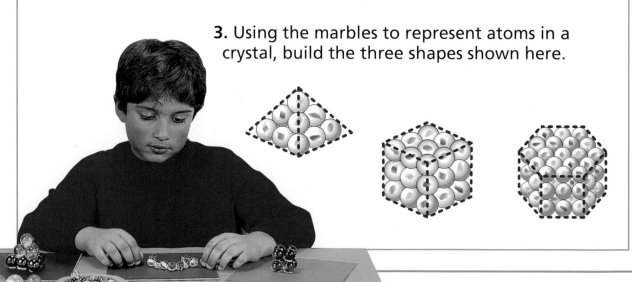

DIFFUSING WATER

1. Cut the piece of plastic so that it will fit in the middle of the container, dividing it in two. You may need an adult's help to do this.

MATERIALS

- a four-sided transparent container
- food coloring in two different colors
- modeling clay
- a small sheet of plastic
- scissors

2. Press strips of modeling clay down the sides of the container and on both sides of the divider. This will make two grooves, which the divider can slide in and out of, and it will help keep water from getting from one side to the other.

3. Check that the divider can slide in and out easily, leaving the modeling clay in place. If the divider sticks to the clay when you pull it out, move it back and forth slightly to widen the groove. Put the divider back in place.

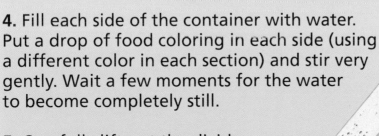

4. Fill each side of the container with water. Put a drop of food coloring in each side (using a different color in each section) and stir very gently. Wait a few moments for the water to become completely still.

5. Carefully lift out the divider, being careful not to disturb the water. Look at the water every few minutes. What happens? Can you explain why this happens?

CHANGES OF STATE

Most substances can change state. They can exist as a solid, a liquid, or a gas. They normally change from one state to another when they are heated or cooled, but changing the pressure can also make substances change state.

Imagine you have a solid substance, such as ice. Heat it, which makes its temperature rise. When it reaches a certain level, the temperature stops rising and the substance begins to turn into a liquid. This temperature is called the substance's melting point.

You keep heating. When all the solid has turned to liquid, the temperature begins to rise again. Eventually the temperature stops rising and the liquid begins to turn into a gas. The temperature at which this happens is called the boiling point. If you keep heating, the temperature stays the same until all the liquid has gone. Then the temperature begins to rise again.

The temperature falls again when you stop heating, and the process

TEMPERATURE CHANGES

1. Pour some warm water into the plastic cup. Put the thermometer into the cup. Make sure that its bulb is completely under the water surface.

2. Stand the cup in the freezer. Return every half hour, and each time gently stir the water with the thermometer. Read the temperature and write it down, together with the time of the reading. Put the thermometer back in the cup each time. Do this until the water is too frozen to stir.

MATERIALS
- water
- a freezer
- a thermometer able to measure below 32° F (0° C)
- a small plastic cup or container
- a large bowl or pan
- a notepad and pencil
- graph paper and colored pencils

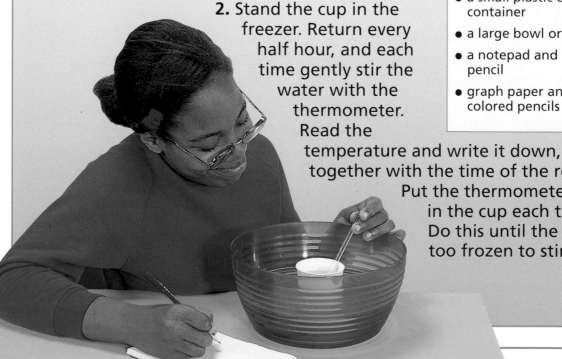

Nitrogen has a very low boiling point and is usually found as a gas. It only becomes a liquid below -324° F (-198° C).

is reversed. The substance changes from a gas to a liquid and back to a solid.

Evaporation is also a change of state from liquid to gas, but it can happen below the boiling point of the substance. For example, puddles of water dry up by evaporation even when the water is quite cool.

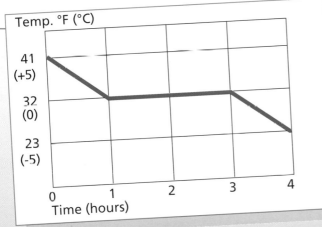

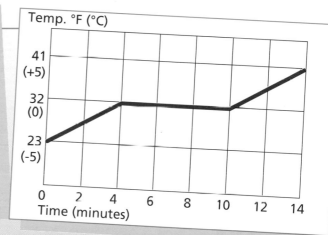

3. When the water has turned to ice and the temperature has fallen to about 41° F (-5° C), take the cup and thermometer out of the freezer.

4. Fill the large bowl or pan with warm water, and put the cup and thermometer into it. Return every two minutes, stirring the water after the ice has melted enough. Take a temperature reading each time, and write it down.

5. Draw line graphs of your two sets of results. Do they look like the ones shown here? (The numbers may not be the same on yours.) Can you explain why the graphs have a horizontal line in the middle?

ELEMENTS AND COMPOUNDS

Scientists have found a total of 109 different types of atoms. Each different type of atom is called an element. Some substances are pure elements. A lump of aluminum is made of just aluminum atoms, and oxygen is made up of just oxygen molecules. Elements are the most simple substances and cannot be broken down into simpler chemicals.

When atoms or molecules of two or more different elements are mixed together, a substance called a mixture is formed. In a mixture, the different atoms or molecules are not joined to each other. For example, air is mainly a mixture of nitrogen gas and oxygen gas.

This is different from a compound, where atoms or molecules of two or more different chemicals are joined together chemically. An example of this is the gas nitrogen dioxide, which is a compound of nitrogen and oxygen. Its molecules contain an atom of nitrogen and two atoms of oxygen.

It is often useful to separate mixtures into their different parts. Chemists do this to find out what chemicals are in a mixture or to extract a chemical they want from the mixture. On the next few pages, we will be looking at some of the methods used by chemists to separate mixtures.

MIXING OIL AND WATER

1. Fill the jar about three-quarters full with water.

2. Add a small amount of cooking oil. You will see that the oil and water don't mix. That is because the oil and water molecules are more attracted to their own kind than to the different ones, so they stay together.

3. Try stirring the oil and water together. At first it looks as though they are mixing, but after a few minutes they separate again.

4. Add some detergent and stir again. The detergent will help the oil and water mix because its molecules attract both the oil and water molecules, and they can mix more easily.

MATERIALS
- cooking oil
- dishwashing detergent
- water
- a spoon
- a jar

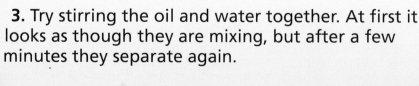

MAGNETIC SEPARATION

MATERIALS
- iron filings
- sand
- a magnet
- a small dish or container

1. Mix some iron filings and sand in the dish.

2. Use the magnet to separate the two parts of this mixture.

ELEMENTS, COMPOUNDS, AND MIXTURES

MATERIALS
- poster board in two colors
- scissors
- a pencil
- a glass or other round object

1. Draw a series of circles on the poster board. Drawing around the glass or other round object will help make good circles.

2. Cut out your circles to make two sets of colored disks. Imagine that disks of one color are atoms of one element, and that disks of the other color are atoms of another element. Use these disks to represent elements, compounds, and mixtures.

3. Divide the disks into their two colors. These piles represent two different elements, each made up of all the same atoms.

4. Now mix the two piles, but without letting the disks touch. This represents a mixture of the two elements.

5. Now join the disks in pairs, one of each color. This represents a compound of the two elements because the elements are chemically joined together.

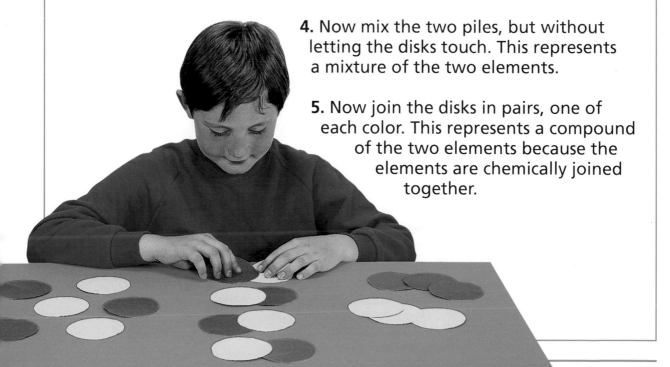

15

SEPARATING MIXTURES

There are several ways of separating mixtures of chemicals into their different parts. One method used to separate a solid and a liquid is called filtration. If you pour a mixture through a filter, liquid will pass through and any solid particles will collect in the filter. Filtration doesn't work if the solid particles are so small that they fit through the tiny holes in the filter paper, or if the mixture is made up of liquids.

One way of separating a mixture of a liquid and tiny particles of solid is to wait a long time! If you leave the mixture very still for several hours (or even days), eventually the solid particles will settle to the bottom of the container, leaving the clear liquid above. This settling process can be speeded up with a machine called a centrifuge.

Chromatography is a way of separating a mixture of dyes, such as inks. Paper chromatography is the simplest type of chromatography. A sample of the mixture is put on a piece of filter paper and a solvent is added. The solvent moves across the filter paper, taking the dyes with it. Some dyes travel farther than others, giving lines or rings of color.

FILTRATION

1. Fill one glass with water and stir in some soil to make a muddy mixture.

MATERIALS
- soil
- filter paper (coffee filters or strong paper towel)
- a funnel
- two glasses or beakers

2. Fold or cut a piece of filter paper so that it fits into the funnel. Rest the funnel in the other glass.

3. Slowly pour the muddy water into the cone. How clean does the filter paper make the water?

PAPER CHROMATOGRAPHY

1. Tape a drinking straw to either side of the tray so that the straws stick up. Insert another straw into the top of each of the first straws to complete two straw supports.

2. Place another straw, or two joined straws, across the top of the supports, inserting the ends into the supports. This will form a bar across the top. Attach a few paper clips to the bar.

3. Fill the tray with water.

4. Cut strips of filter paper or blotting paper long enough to reach from the bar into the tray.

5. Find a few different colored pens, inks, and food colorings to test. For colored pens, draw an inky blob about 1 in. (2.5 cm) from the end of a strip. For colored liquids, use a small drop the same way. Use a separate strip for each test.

DID YOU KNOW?

Forensic scientists use chromatography to test whether chemicals, such as paint flecks, from the scene of a crime match those found on a suspect.

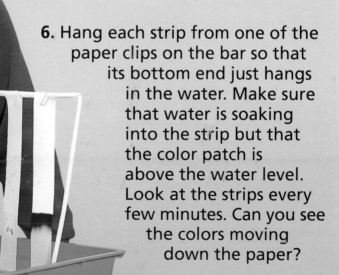

6. Hang each strip from one of the paper clips on the bar so that its bottom end just hangs in the water. Make sure that water is soaking into the strip but that the color patch is above the water level. Look at the strips every few minutes. Can you see the colors moving down the paper?

SOLUTIONS

When you stir sugar into a cup of coffee or tea, the sugar seems to disappear, although the overall volume increases. Where does it go? The answer is that it breaks up into small groups of atoms, far too small to see, that mix in with the water molecules in the coffee or tea. A mixture like this is called a solution. We say that the sugar has dissolved in the water. The water is called the solvent and the sugar is called the solute.

Water is a very good solvent. It can dissolve many different solids, gases, and other liquids. Think about what happens when you open a bottle of soda. The fizz is made by the carbon dioxide gas that is dissolved in the drink. When you open the bottle, the gas begins to come out of the solution, forming bubbles.

Not all substances dissolve in water. Metals, china, wood, and other solids go in and out of water all the time without dissolving. Also, think about washing dishes. Plain water does not wash away oil. Soap and detergent help because their molecules cling to

MAKING SOLUTIONS

You will find that temperature makes a difference to how easily a solute can dissolve. In the case of solids that dissolve in liquids, the solubility usually increases with higher temperatures.

MATERIALS
- teaspoon
- sugar
- two glasses of water

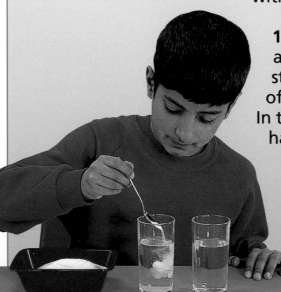

1. Fill a glass with cold water. Gradually add sugar, a level teaspoon at a time, and stir until the sugar dissolves. Keep count of the number of spoons of sugar you use. In the end, no more sugar will dissolve. You have made a saturated solution.

2. Repeat step **1**, using exactly the same amount of water, but this time use warm water. How much sugar dissolved this time? What difference did the temperature of the solvent make to the amount of solute that could be dissolved in it?

the water and the oil, helping to dissolve it. Some solvents, called organic solvents, can dissolve oily substances. For example, you use mineral spirit to wash oil paint from a paintbrush.

Fish breathe by extracting the oxygen that is dissolved in water. They filter the water through gills under the flaps behind their heads. Their gills provide their bodies with oxygen, just as our lungs do when they extract oxygen from the air.

AIR AND SOLUTIONS

Compare this project with the last one. The amount of air dissolved in the water reduces as the temperature of the water rises. That is because the solubility of a gas reduces as the temperature rises.

MATERIALS
- a large bowl
- a glass or beaker

1. Fill the glass with cold water, and put it into the bowl.

2. Fill the bowl with enough warm water to surround the glass but not to overflow into it.

3. Can you see bubbles forming in the water? These are bubbles of air, coming out of the solution as the water warms up.

DISTILLATION

Sometimes you need to separate a solution into its solvent and the solute in it. For example, if you have some salty water, you might want to separate it into fresh water and salt. A simple way to do this is by evaporation. The solution is heated so that the solvent evaporates, leaving the solute behind.

Unfortunately, if you evaporate a solution, you lose the solvent into the air. Sometimes you want to keep it. To do this, you use a process called distillation. Distillation starts with evaporation, but the evaporated solvent is condensed, which means it is cooled down again so that it turns back to liquid. In a laboratory, the solvent is cooled in a condenser. This has a central tube where the solvent enters, surrounded by a pipe that contains cold water.

Distillation is also used to separate a mixture of liquids that have different boiling points. The process is called fractional distillation. The mixture is heated until its temperature reaches the boiling point of one liquid, which then evaporates and is collected by condensing it. Then the temperature is raised until it reaches the boiling point of the next liquid, and so on. Crude oil is separated into different types of oil by fractional distillation.

At this salt works in the Canary Islands, the seawater evaporates off the salt pans during the day. The salt deposits left behind are then collected and refined.

SALTWATER DISTILLATION

1. Stir several teaspoons of salt into a glass of warm water. Taste a drop of the water to see how salty it is.

2. Pour the water into the saucepan. Stand the small cup or egg cup in the center of the pan, making sure that the cup's rim is above the surface of the water in the pan.

3. Cut a circle of foil about 4 in. (10 cm) wider than the top of the pan. Place the foil over the pan, folding the sides down. Tie string around the pan just below the rim to keep the foil in place. Cut off the loose ends of string.

4. Press a finger gently in the center of the foil to make a dip in the middle. Put a few ice cubes on top of the foil.

5. Ask an adult to help you with this stage. Put the pan carefully onto the stove. Turn the stove on at a low setting. After a while you should hear the water begin to boil. After a few minutes of boiling, turn off the stove and allow the pan to cool.

6. Remove the foil. Is there some water in the cup? Taste it. What has happened to it? Taste the water in the pan too. What has happened to it? Can you explain how the distillation has happened?

MATERIALS

- water
- salt
- a teaspoon
- a glass or beaker
- a medium-sized saucepan
- a small cup or egg cup
- aluminum foil
- scissors
- string
- ice cubes

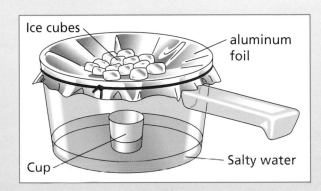

Ice cubes — aluminum foil — Cup — Salty water

METALS

Elements are grouped together according to their properties in a large chart called the periodic table. Although the elements listed have many different properties, they are all either metals or nonmetals.

All metals except mercury are solids at room temperature. Most of them are gray. They are shiny when cut, but most corrode on the outside. Metals are useful for making things because they can be cut, bent, and hammered into shape. They can also be stretched into thin wires. Metals are also good conductors of heat and electricity, which means that heat and electricity can easily flow through them.

The most common metal that we make use of is iron. Examples of things made from iron are drainpipes, manhole covers, and engine parts. Other important metals are copper, aluminum, and zinc. An alloy is a mixture of two different metals. For example, bronze is a mixture of copper and tin.

Steel is mostly iron with some carbon added to it. It is much stronger than iron and is used to construct buildings and bridges and for making tools, cars, and many machine parts.

FLAME TESTS

You will need an adult to help you with this project.

1. Straighten a paper clip and push one end well into a cork. This tool is for holding samples in a flame. Always hold it by the cork.

2. File each metal sample over a piece of paper and collect a small amount of filings from each.

3. Light the candle.

4. Dip the wire end of the sampling tool in water and then into one of your samples. Some filings will attach themselves to the tip of the sampling tool.

5. Hold the end over the top of the candle flame. You should see a colored flash in the flame. What color do you get?

6. Try the flame test on your other metal samples.

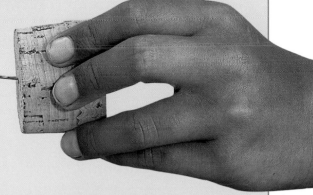

7. Try some flame tests on other substances, such as salt or bicarbonate of soda. Do you get colored flames? This might show that the substance contains a metal. For example, salt contains the metal sodium.

MATERIALS

- a paper clip
- a cork
- different metal samples, such as steel, brass, and copper nails
- a small metalworking file
- a container of water
- some sheets of paper
- a candle
- safety matches
- goggles
- salt
- bicarbonate of soda (baking powder)

WARNING!

- Wearing goggles will protect your eyes from metal filings and sparks.

- Make sure an adult is present when you are using matches.

NONMETALS

Most of the elements are metals, but about twenty elements are not. They are called nonmetals. The properties of nonmetals are quite different from those of metals. They are all either solids or gases at room temperature, except bromine, which is a liquid.

The solids are not very strong. They snap easily, so they cannot be easily shaped as metals can. Except for carbon, when it is in the form of graphite, they are poor conductors of electricity. All non-metals are poor conductors of heat.

The most common nonmetals are carbon, hydrogen, oxygen, nitrogen, silicon, sulfur, and chlorine.

The element carbon can exist in two forms—diamond and graphite, the gray substance used to make pencil leads. However, carbon is found in compounds in almost all natural substances. Compounds of carbon are also used to make plastics and other synthetic products. The elements oxygen and nitrogen are the two gases that make up nearly 99 percent of the air in the earth's atmosphere.

There is more hydrogen in the universe than any other element. This red cloud, the Lagoon Nebula, is made of hydrogen gas. As well as being one of the most common elements in living things, hydrogen is the main ingredient of water.

DID YOU KNOW?
Bags of potato chips are filled with nitrogen rather than air. This keeps oxygen from reacting with the chips and making them stale.

All animals need to breathe oxygen to live.

Nonmetals combine to form other important chemicals, including water (a compound of hydrogen and oxygen), ammonia (hydrogen and nitrogen), sulfuric acid (hydrogen, oxygen, and sulfur), and carbon dioxide (carbon and oxygen). They also combine with metals to form chemicals called salts, such as common salt (sodium and chlorine) and chalk (calcium, carbon, and oxygen).

TESTING CARBON DIOXIDE

You can test for the presence of carbon dioxide by adding it to limewater because it will turn the limewater cloudy. Powdered lime and limewater can both be bought from pharmacists or from some lawn and garden stores. To make limewater from powdered lime, ask an adult to dissolve a small amount in some water.

MATERIALS

- a large plastic bottle of soda water
- a balloon
- a straw
- a glass or beaker
- limewater or powdered lime

1. Pour an inch or so of limewater into the glass or beaker. Rest the straw in the limewater.

2. Pull the neck of the balloon over the cap and neck of the soda water bottle. Carefully unscrew the bottle top by turning it gently through the skin of the balloon. The gas released will be captured in the balloon.

3. Take the balloon off the bottle, pinching the neck as you do so, to keep the gas from escaping.

4. Still pinching the balloon with one hand, put the lower part of its neck over the top of the straw, and hold it in place with the other hand.

5. Release the hand that is pinching the balloon, and squeeze the middle of the balloon. This will make the gas bubble into the limewater. What else happens?

ACIDS AND ALKALIS

When you take a bite from a slice of lemon, you get a very sour, sharp, taste. The taste is caused by a chemical in the lemon called citric acid. You get a similar taste from vinegar, which also contains acid. Common acids used by chemists are sulfuric acid, nitric acid, and hydrochloric acid. These acids can eat away at metals and burn your skin and clothes.

Many common chemicals, such as baking powder and cleaning fluids, dissolve in water to make chemicals called alkalis. Alkalis feel soapy on your fingers. Alkalis are related to acids because an alkali neutralizes an acid. Substances that are neither acids nor alkalis are neutral substances.

You can find out whether a chemical is an acid or an alkali by using another

DID YOU KNOW?

Combining an acid and an alkali creates a neutralization reaction. Farmers often spread lime on their fields to neutralize the acidity in their soil.

NATURAL INDICATORS

Most indicators are found naturally in plants. Red cabbage is a useful indicator that changes color when added to acids and alkalis.

MATERIALS
- red cabbage leaves
- a bowl
- water
- a wooden spoon
- a strainer
- a pitcher
- four or five small bottles or jars
- vinegar
- bicarbonate of soda (baking powder)
- milk of magnesia
- rainwater

1. Ask an adult to help you with this step. Tear a few leaves of red cabbage into small strips. Put them in a bowl, pour in about two cups of boiling water from a teakettle, and stir.

2. Allow the liquid to cool and then strain it into a pitcher. This is your indicator. Throw away the used cabbage leaves.

chemical called an indicator, which changes color when an acid or an alkali is added to it. Some acids and alkalis have a much greater effect than others. For example, citric acid is weak, but hydrochloric acid is strong.

Universal indicator is a special indicator made of a mixture of dyes. It uses different colors to show the strength of an acid or alkali. The strength is measured on the pH scale, which goes from 1 (strong acid) through 7 (neutral) to 14 (strong alkali).

Acid rain is made when sulfur dioxide from burning fuels collects in the atmosphere and falls back to Earth in rainwater. This can cause great harm to plants, water, and buildings. The effect of acid rain on trees can be seen here.

3. Half fill a small bottle with vinegar (a weak acid), and another with bicarbonate of soda (a weak alkali) dissolved in water.

4. Add a very small amount of indicator to each bottle, and watch the color change. What colors do you get?

5. Repeat steps 3 and 4, using milk of magnesia, which is a stronger alkali. What happens this time?

6. Collect and test some rainwater. Compare it with tap water and boiled, cooled water. Is there any difference among them?

7. Put some indicator in an empty bottle, and add some acid. Then add an alkali. Can you make the indicator go back to neutral? Try again, adding an alkali first and then an acid.

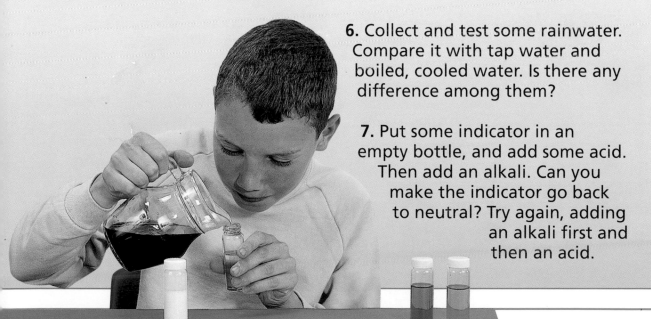

CHEMICAL REACTIONS

When you mix some different chemicals together, nothing happens. You simply get a mixture of the two chemicals. But when you mix other chemicals, they react with each other, and new chemicals are made. This is called a chemical reaction. The original chemicals are called reactants, and the new chemicals are called products.

When you think of chemical reactions, you might imagine them as always happening in test tubes in the laboratory. They do, of course, but many chemical reactions are happening around you all the time. Everyday reactions happen in cooking, cleaning and all the time in your body and in plants.

Chemical reactions are often written down as a word equation, which shows the reactants and the products. An arrow shows which way the reaction goes. Here is an example:

hydrochloric acid + sodium hydroxide $\longrightarrow$ sodium chloride + water

A SIMPLE REACTION

The end of the funnel must be small enough to fit in the tube.

1. Ask an adult to cut two holes in the lid of the large jar, just large enough to fit the tubing through.

2. Put a teaspoonful of bicarbonate of soda in the jar. Put the lid on the jar.

MATERIALS
- a small glass or jar
- a large jar with a lid
- a tray or dish with sides
- vinegar
- a teaspoon
- plastic tubing, $3/8$ in. (1 cm) wide
- a small funnel
- modeling clay
- bicarbonate of soda (baking powder)

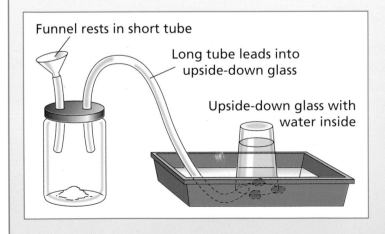

Funnel rests in short tube

Long tube leads into upside-down glass

Upside-down glass with water inside

3. Cut two pieces of plastic tubing—one about 4 in. (10 cm) long and the other about 16 in. (40 cm) long. Put one end of each tube into the holes in the jar's lid.

4. Fill the tray with water and stand it next to the jar.

This reaction is called a permanent reaction because the products (sodium chloride and water) do not react with each other. The reaction cannot be reversed. Some reactions can be reversed: nitrogen + hydrogen = ammonia is an example of this. The = sign tells us that a reaction is reversible.

When a substance burns, a chemical reaction is taking place. The reactants are the substance itself and oxygen in the air.

5. Press three blobs of modeling clay onto the rim of the glass. Hold the glass under the water and lift its base so that it is upside down, resting on the blobs and with water trapped inside. This is your collecting beaker.

6. Push the end of the long tube under the water and into the beaker.

7. Put the funnel in the short tube and pour in a few drops of vinegar. Gently shake the jar, and put your finger over the short tube. Watch the reaction between the two chemicals. What happens inside the collecting beaker? Where do you think the gas comes from?

8. Eventually, the gas stops flowing, because one of the chemicals has been used up. Try adding some more vinegar. Does the reaction start again? Keep adding vinegar until no more gas is created. Can you explain why the gas stops being produced?

BURNING

Burning (which is also called combustion) is a common chemical reaction. Burning happens when a substance reacts with oxygen in the air. We use burning to create heat for cooking and heating, to make light, and to make movement in engines.

Burning does not start by itself. If it did, things would be bursting into flames all the time. To make something burn, you need to give it energy by heating it up. For example, you need to make a hot spark to ignite the burner on a gas stove. The burning reaction creates heat as it happens, so once it has started it keeps going. A burning reaction that creates heat is called an exothermic reaction. Some reactions use up energy as they happen. These reactions are called endothermic reactions.

OXYGEN IN THE AIR

1. Stand a candle in the center of a shallow dish, fixing it in place with modeling clay.

2. Put three blobs of modeling clay around the candle. Rest the glass upside down over the candle. It will sit on the blobs of clay, so that there is a gap under the rim.

MATERIALS
- a candle
- a shallow dish
- modeling clay
- a glass or beaker
- safety matches

3. Fill the dish with water.

WARNING
- Make sure an adult is present when you are using matches.

4. Lift the glass, and ask an adult to light the candle for you. Replace the glass. Eventually, the candle will go out. What happens to the water level? Which of the gases that make up the air has been used up? Think about the three things needed for burning to take place.

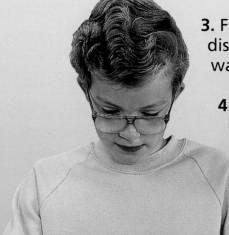

For burning to take place, three things are needed: a substance that burns, a supply of oxygen, and a supply of heat (which is normally made by the reaction itself). If any of the these things is removed, the burning stops.

Because fires need both a supply of heat and a supply of oxygen to burn, firefighters can stop fires in two ways. They pour on water to reduce the temperature, as they are doing here, or they cover the flames with foam to cut off the oxygen supply.

A TEMPERATURE DROP

You can create an endothermic reaction, which uses energy as it happens.

MATERIALS
- vinegar
- bicarbonate of soda (baking soda)
- a thermometer
- a small bottle or jar
- a dishpan

1. Pour about an inch (2–3 cm) of vinegar into the bottle or jar.

2. Put the thermometer into the vinegar. Wait a few seconds for the reading to settle and then write down the temperature.

3. Pour a teaspoon of bicarbonate of soda into the bottle, and gently shake the tube to mix the bicarbonate of soda and vinegar. (This stage should be done over a dishpan or sink to catch any overflow.)

4. Watch the thermometer as the chemical reaction happens. What happens to the temperature?

CORROSION

If you have ever accidentally left a shiny steel object, such as a pair of scissors, outside in the rain, you will have noticed that the bare metal soon loses it shine. After a few days, it is covered with red-brown flakes. This is caused by a chemical reaction called corrosion. The red-brown coating on the steel is called rust. Eventually, the steel will be completely eaten away.

Corrosion happens when a metal reacts with oxygen and often water (either water vapor in the air or rainwater). The chemical formed is an oxide of the metal, often combined with water. For example, rust is a compound of iron oxide and water (remember that steel is made mostly of iron).

Because steel is so widely used for making cars and trucks, and in building, rusting is an expensive problem. There are several ways to reduce rusting. One method is to coat the metal surface with a protective layer, such as paint.

Some metals, such as magnesium, corrode very quickly. Other metals, such as gold and silver, corrode much more slowly.

DID YOU KNOW?

Steel objects can be protected from corrosion by covering them with a layer of zinc. The air reacts with the zinc instead of with the iron in the steel, so the steel is protected from rust. This process is called galvanizing.

WHAT CAUSES RUSTING?

1. Number your bottles from one to six and fill them as follows:

1. add a small amount of tap water
2. fill up with tap water
3. fill up with boiled water that has been allowed to cool for a few minutes
4. fill up with tap water with a few pinches of salt dissolved in it
5. fill up with cooking oil
6. leave empty

2. Drop a steel nail into each tube. Put lids on the bottle with boiled water and the empty bottle.

3. Look at the bottles every day for a week, and write down what has happened in each tube. Which nail rusts first? Which nails don't rust? Can you explain your results?

4. Using the mixture that caused the most rusting, see if other metals corrode in the same way as iron and steel. Try copper nails and zinc-covered screws.

RATES OF REACTION

What is the difference between the reaction that makes fireworks explode and the one that makes rust form on iron? The answer is that the explosion happens very quickly and the rusting happens very slowly. The speed of a reaction is called the rate of reaction. There are several ways of changing the rate of a reaction to make it happen faster or slower.

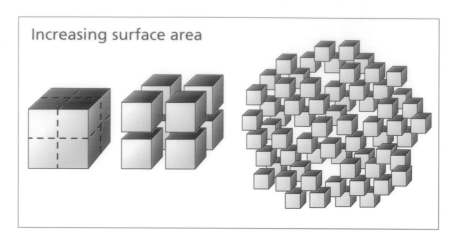

Increasing surface area

Breaking a solid reactant into smaller pieces will make a reaction faster. That is because the surface area is increased, allowing more contact between the reactants.

Increasing the temperature of the reactants increases the rate of a reaction. This happens because the particles in the reactants move around more quickly when they are hotter. This makes them more likely to bump into one another and react together. On the other hand, cooling the reactants reduces the rate of reaction. Refrigerators keep food fresh for longer because they slow the reaction between the food and the air around it.

Increasing the concentration of the reactants also increases the rate of reaction. For example, if one reactant is a solution, making the solution stronger by using twice as much solute will double the rate of the reaction.

In controlled explosions such as this one, a fast chemical reaction releases a huge volume of gases at the right moment.

CHANGING RATES OF REACTION

MATERIALS

- two small bottles or jars
- two bowls or trays with high sides
- a small funnel
- two balloons
- vinegar
- bicarbonate of soda (baking powder)
- water
- ice cubes

1. Pour a very small amount of vinegar into both of the bottles.

2. Using the funnel, pour a level teaspoon of baking powder into both balloons. Shake it to the bottom of the balloon.

3. Carefully stretch the neck of one balloon over the neck of one of the bottles, leaving the bulb of the balloon to flop to one side. Make sure the baking powder stays in the bottom of the balloon and doesn't fall into the bottle. Do the same with the other bottle and balloon.

4. Stand one bottle in a bowl of melting ice cubes and the other in a bowl of hot water. Wait a few minutes to let the vinegar change temperature.

5. Now lift the balloons at the same time so that the baking powder drops into the vinegar. Which balloon inflates most? What does this tell you about the effect of temperature on the rate of a reaction?

6. Repeat the experiment from the beginning. This time do not stand the jars in trays. Instead, add some water to one of the jars to dilute the vinegar. Which balloon inflates most this time? Why do you think this happens?

CATALYSTS

On the last two pages you saw that changing the temperature, the concentration of the reactants, and the surface area of a solid reactant all change the rate of a reaction. The final way of changing the rate of reaction is to add a chemical called a catalyst. The catalyst takes part in the reaction, and helps it to happen. But when the reaction has finished, the catalyst ends up unchanged.

You have catalysts in your body. These natural catalysts are called enzymes. For example, enzymes in your saliva help break down your food into simple chemicals that your body can digest.

FERMENTATION

Yeast is an enzyme used in brewing to make sugar and water react to produce alcohol and carbon dioxide gas.

1. Make a saturated solution of sugar by dissolving as much sugar as you can in a pitcher of warm water.

2. Divide the solution between two jars. Add one level teaspoon of bakers' yeast to one of the jars.

3. Stand the jars on the tray and put them in a warm place. Check them every day to see what happens. The solution with the yeast in it will produce bubbles because it is fermenting.

4. When the reactions have stopped, put some of the yeast solution into a saucer. Put the saucer on a windowsill and leave it until the liquid has evaporated. What is left in the saucer?

MATERIALS
- a pitcher
- sugar
- dried bakers' yeast
- water
- a teaspoon
- two jars or beakers
- a plastic tray
- a saucer

Car engines make exhaust gases that contain harmful chemicals and pollute the atmosphere. Most cars have a device called a catalytic converter in their exhaust systems. The pollutants from the engine go through thousands of tiny holes coated with catalysts. The reactions that take place turn the pollutants into less harmful chemicals.

Have you ever wondered how a photographic film records a picture? It contains chemicals that react only when light hits the film. The more light that hits, the faster the reaction happens. This is called a photochemical reaction.

5. Add the contents of the saucer to the jar containing the plain sugar and water solution. Does it cause fermentation to start? If it does, it must still be yeast. It has taken part in the fermentation reaction, but has been left unchanged at the end. It has acted as a catalyst.

ELECTROLYSIS

As we discovered on page 8, an ion is an atom that has lost or gained one or more electrons. Electrons have a tiny negative electric charge. In a complete atom, the negative charge of the electrons is equaled by the positive charge of the protons in the atom's nucleus. When an atom becomes an ion by *losing* electrons, it becomes positively charged and is called a cation. If it *gains* electrons, it becomes negatively charged, and is called an anion.

Electroplating uses electrolysis to cover a metal object with a thin layer of another metal. The object is the cathode, and metal ions in the liquid form a coating over it. Jewelry made from an inexpensive metal, such as steel, can be electroplated with a layer of gold to make it more attractive. The metal sheets (right) have just been copper-plated and will be used to make electrical circuits.

ELECTRIC LIQUID

1. Cut a piece of cardboard to fit over the container. Ask an adult to make two holes in the cardboard, about 1 in. (2 –3 cm) apart, just large enough to hold the carbon rods.

2. Cut a piece of wire about 3 ft. (1 m) long, and bare about 1 in. (2.5 cm) of the wire at each end. Wrap the center of the wire around the compass about ten times. Then connect one end of the wire to a terminal of the battery, and the other end to one of the carbon rods, using alligator clips.

3. Cut another piece of wire, bare the ends, and use alligator clips to connect it to the other battery terminal and the other carbon rod.

MATERIALS
- a piece of stiff cardboard
- a plastic or glass container
- two carbon rods or pencil leads
- insulated copper wire
- four alligator clips
- a 6-volt battery
- a compass
- water

You can separate anions and cations by a process called electrolysis. Two electrodes are connected to a battery and placed into a liquid containing the ions. The negative anions are attracted to the electrode connected to the positive terminal of the battery (called the anode). The positive cations are connected to the electrode connected to the negative terminal of the battery (called the cathode). When they arrive at the electrodes, the ions will gain or lose electrons and turn back into atoms.

One use of electrolysis is to extract elements from their compounds. For example, sodium can be extracted from common salt by electrolysis of the molten salt. The sodium cations move to the negative electrode, where they gain electrons to become sodium atoms.

In the process of electrolysis, the cations move toward the cathode, where they gain electrons. The anions are attracted to the anode, where they lose electrons. They turn back into atoms, and a new substance is formed.

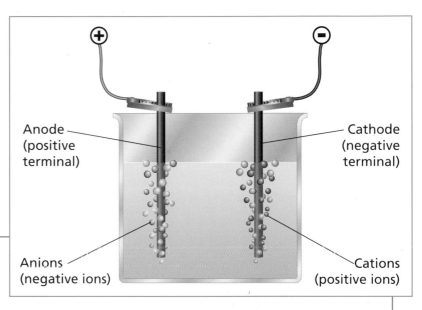

Anode (positive terminal)

Cathode (negative terminal)

Anions (negative ions)

Cations (positive ions)

4. Push the carbon rods through the holes into the container. Make sure that the rods don't touch the bottom of the container or each other.

5. Fill the container with water. What happens to the compass? If it moves, an electric current is flowing through the water. Look closely at the electrodes. Can you see bubbles of gas forming? Which gas do you think there is more of?

REACTIVITY

Sodium and gold are both metals. So why is it that outside the laboratory you never see sodium metal as an element, but you see plenty of gold? The answer is that sodium is very reactive, so it always combines with other elements to form compounds. Gold doesn't form compounds and is always found as an element. It has always been used to make precious objects, because it is unreactive and doesn't corrode.

The reactivity series is a list of commonly found metals in order of how reactive they are. Potassium is the most reactive, and gold is the least reactive.

Reactivity series
Potassium
Sodium
Calcium
Magnesium
Aluminum
Zinc
Iron
Tin
Lead
Copper
Mercury
Silver
Platinum
Gold

A SIMPLE BATTERY

1. Cut 10 strips of aluminum foil to the same size as the copper strips.

2. Repeat this process with the blotting paper, but this time make the strips a a little bit larger than the copper ones.

3. Cut a piece of wire about 3 ft. (1 m) long and bare about 1 in. (2.5 cm) of the wire at each end. Wrap the middle of the wire around a compass about ten times. Tape one end of the wire onto the cardboard and place the compass next to it.

MATERIALS

- 10 copper strips 3 in. X 1 in. (7.5 cm x 3 cm)
- aluminum foil
- blotting paper or filter paper
- scissors
- tape
- insulated copper wire
- a compass
- a piece of stiff cardboard 5 in. X 5 in. (12 cm x 12 cm)
- salt
- water
- a small dish or bowl

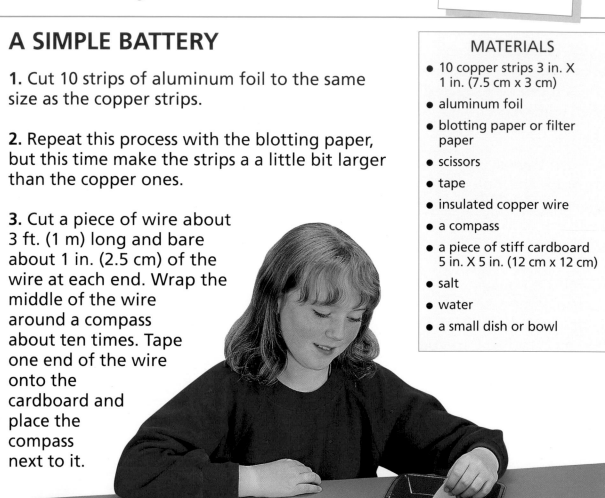

The difference in reactivity is used in cells and batteries to produce electricity. A simple cell has two different electrodes. They are put into a paste called electrolyte, which contains ions. The negative ions react with the electrode with higher reactivity and release a stream of electrons. This makes an electric current.

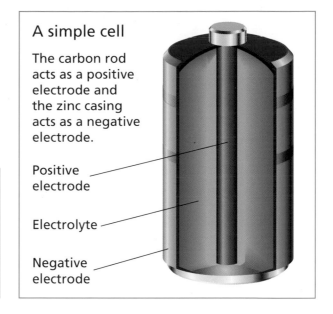

A simple cell

The carbon rod acts as a positive electrode and the zinc casing acts as a negative electrode.

Positive electrode

Electrolyte

Negative electrode

4. Put some warm water in the dish, and stir in salt until no more will dissolve.

5. Put a copper strip on top of the bare wire on the cardboard. Dip a blotting paper strip in the salt solution and put it on top of the copper strip. Put a foil strip on top of the blotting paper. Now add another copper strip, another dipped blotting paper strip, and another foil strip. Keep going in this order until you have used up all the strips.

6. Turn the compass so that the needle lies in the same direction as the coil of wire around it. Now touch the spare wire against the top foil disk. Does the compass needle twitch? That is because you have made a battery with your stack of strips. Can you see the cells in it, each made up of two different metals separated by an electrolyte?

CHEMICALS FROM OIL

Oil is a fossil fuel. It is made from the remains of dead sea creatures that have been buried under layers of rock for millions of years. The oil that is pumped out of the ground at oil wells is called crude oil.

Crude oil is made up of many different compounds, all of which contain hydrogen and carbon. Some have very simple molecules, which contain just hydrogen and carbon atoms. These are called hydrocarbons. Other compounds in crude oil contain molecules with hundreds of atoms.

Crude oil is separated into its different chemicals by fractional distillation (see page 20). More than three fourths of the compounds in crude oil go to make fuels.

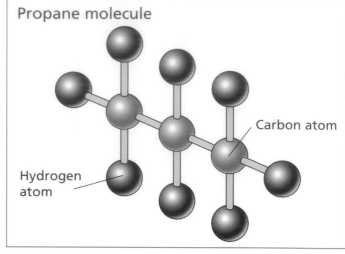

Propane molecule

Carbon atom

Hydrogen atom

One example of a hydrocarbon is propane, the molecules of which contain three carbon atoms and eight hydrogen atoms.

Gases such as methane and butane, and the liquids kerosene and petroleum, are all fuels made from crude oil. The compounds with larger molecules go to make bitumen and lubricating oil. Some of the compounds are used to make other chemicals, such as plastics, fertilizers, and dyes.

Plastics are made by joining small hydrocarbon molecules, called monomers, into very large molecules, called polymers. A polymer may contain tens of thousands of carbon atoms in a long chain.

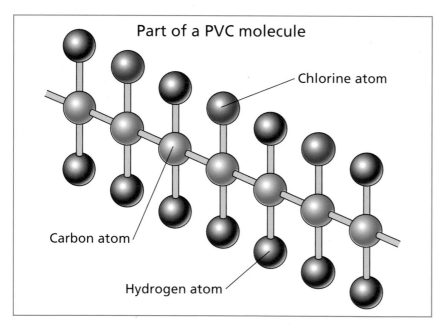

Part of a PVC molecule

Chlorine atom

Carbon atom

Hydrogen atom

MAKING A PLASTIC

You can produce your own plastic by making a polymer with milk and vinegar.

1. Ask an adult to warm the milk in the saucepan, and take it off the heat before it boils.

2. Add three tablespoons of vinegar to the milk and stir it in. The white solid that appears in the liquid is called casein, which is a natural polymer.

3. Put the muslin over the bowl and strain the liquid through it. It will go through slowly, leaving the casein behind on the cloth.

4. Scrape the casein off the cloth and make it into a lump. Mold it into some small shapes, such as cubes and spheres. Leave the shapes to solidify for a few days. The casein will harden into solid, plasticlike material as its molecules bond tightly together.

TYPES OF PLASTICS

Plastics are being used more and more to make things that used to be made of metal or wood. They are often cheaper, easier to shape, and longer lasting. Plastics do have disadvantages, however. Except for the few plastics that are biodegradable, they do not decompose when thrown away.

We found out on pages 42–43 that plastics are polymers, made by joining small molecules together into long chains. Different types of plastic are made by joining different monomers together. Polyethylene, for instance, is made by polymerizing the gas ethylene.

Types of plastic	Used for
Polyethylene	Plastic bags
Polystyrene	Plastic pens and packing materials
PVC	Wiring and hoses
Nylon	Fabrics and pen nibs
Acrylic	Safety glass
Melamine	Picnic plates and cups
Acetate	Paints
Teflon	Nonstick surfaces

Plastics can even be used to make roads. Because these polystyrene blocks are so light, the road is easy and cheap to build.

Like other substances, different plastics have properties that make them useful for varying purposes. Some plastics, such as polyethylene and nylon, get soft when they are warmed and harden when they cool. They are called thermoplastics and are easy to mold into shape. Thermoset plastics set hard when they are made and stay hard when they are heated.

THERMOPLASTICS

1. Put the glass or beaker on the tray and fill it with hot water.

2. Press a piece of plastic cutlery down on the tray and notice how flexible it feels. Put the cutlery into the hot water and leave it there for a minute.

3. Take the cutlery out and press it down on the tray. Does it feel softer or bend more easily? Let it cool down again. Does it get hard? If it does, it is a thermoplastic.

MATERIALS
- a large glass or beaker
- a tray
- hot water
- plastic cutlery (knife, fork, or spoon)
- a selection of other plastic objects

DID YOU KNOW?

Most plastics come out of the factories where they are made in the form of fingertip-sized pellets. The pellets are melted before they are shaped into plastic products.

4. Repeat steps **1** to **3**, using other plastic objects. Do you get different results?

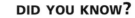

45

GLOSSARY

Atom A tiny "building block" from which all substances are made.

Boiling The change of state from a liquid to a gas.

Burning A chemical reaction, which happens when a substance reacts with oxygen.

Catalyst A chemical that changes the rate of a reaction without being changed itself.

Centrifuge A machine that rotates at high speed, separating solids from liquids, or liquids from other liquids.

Chromatography A method of separating a mixture of dyes.

Compound A substance made from particles of two or more elements joined together.

Condensation The change of state from a gas to a liquid.

Crystal A solid in which the particles fit together in a regular pattern.

Density The amount of substance in a certain volume. A volume of a more dense substance weighs more than the same volume of a less dense substance.

Distillation A method of separating a solution into its solvent and solute.

Electrolysis A method of separating ions using electricity.

Electron A tiny particle that is part of an atom. A stream of electrons makes up an electric current.

Element A substance made from only one type of atom.

Evaporation The change of state from a liquid to a gas at a temperature below the boiling point.

Filtration A method of separating a solid and a liquid.

Forensic scientist A scientist who carries out tests used by police and in courts of law.

Freezing The change of state from a liquid to a solid.

Indicator A chemical that changes color to show whether another chemical is an acid or an alkali.

Ion An electrically charged atom, which is made when an atom gains or loses an electron.

Melting The change of state from a solid to a liquid.

Mixture A substance made from particles of two or more elements or compounds mixed, but not joined, together.

Molecule A group of atoms joined together.

Monomer One of the small molecules that link together to form polymers.

Nucleus The particle at the center of an atom, made up of neutrons and protons.

Polymer A large molecule made from many monomers linked together in a chain.

Reactants The chemicals that take part in a chemical reaction.

Reactive Showing a reaction.

Solute The substance that dissolves in a solvent to form a solution.

Solvent The liquid that dissolves a solute to form a solution.

Synthetic A substance produced artificially (rather than a natural substance).

FURTHER INFORMATION

Fitgerald, Karen. *A Story of Iron* (First Book). Danbury, CT: Franklin Watts, 1997.

———. *A Story of Nitrogen* (First Book). Danbury, CT: Franklin Watts, 1997.

———. *A Story of Oxygen* (First Book). Danbury, CT: Franklin Watts, 1996.

Mebane, Robert C. *Adventures with Atoms and Molecules, Book V: Chemistry Experiments for Young People* (Adventures With Science). Springfield, NJ: Enslow Publishers, 1995.

———. *Plastics and Polymers* (Everyday Material Science Experiments). New York: 21st Century Books, 1995.

Newmark, Ann. *Chemistry* (Eyewitness Science). New York: Dorling Kindersley, 1993.

Newton, David E. *The Chemical Elements* (Venture). Danbury, CT: Franklin Watts, 1994.

Vancleave, Janice. *Janice Vancleave's Microscopes and Magnifying Lenses: Mind-Boggling Chemistry and Biology Experiments You Can Turn into Science fair Projects.* New York: John Wiley & Sons, 1993.

———. *Janice Vancleave's Molecules* (Spectacular Science Projects). New York: John Wiley & Sons, 1992.

ANSWERS TO QUESTIONS

Answers to questions posed in the projects.

Pages 4–5 The burning candle uses up oxygen gas in the bottle. This reduces the air pressure inside the bottle. The higher pressure outside the bottle pushes the egg in.

Pages 10–11 The particles of the food coloring are moving about randomly together with the water molecules. They gradually move through the water until it all becomes one color.

Pages 12–13 During the time that the line is horizontal, the energy that goes into or leaves the water causes a change of state instead of a change in temperature.

Pages 18–19 The warmer the solvent, the more solid solute dissolves in it.

Pages 20–21 When the salty water in the pan boils, the water vapor formed rises up. It hits the foil, cools, turns back to water and drips into the cup, making fresh water. The salt is left in the pan.

Page 25 The limewater turns milky, which tells us that the gas is carbon dioxide.

Pages 28–29 The gas that bubbles into the jar has been made by the reaction. The gas stops being produced because the reaction stops when all the bicarbonate of soda is used up.

Pages 30–31 The water level rises because oxygen in the air is used up by the burning.
The temperature should drop slightly because energy is taken in by the reaction.

Pages 34–35 The reaction speeds up when the temperature rises.
When the vinegar is diluted, there is less acid to take part in the reaction, so it slows down.

Pages 38–39 The gases are oxygen and hydrogen.

INDEX